# STECK-VAUGHN
# TARGET Spelling 360

Margaret Scarborough
Mary F. Brigham
Teresa A. Miller

## STECK-VAUGHN
### COMPANY
A Subsidiary of National Education Corporation

# Table of Contents

## About the Authors

Margaret M. Scarborough teaches at Elizabeth Seawell Elementary School in Chapel Hill, North Carolina. Her master's degree was conferred by the University of North Carolina. Ms. Scarborough has taught kindergarten through sixth-grade students with special learning needs. She works collaboratively with regular classroom teachers, remedial reading teachers, speech and language pathologists, and behavioral therapists. She is a member of the Learning Disabilities Association of North Carolina and past president of the Orange County Association for Children and Adults with Learning Disabilities.

Mary F. Brigham is principal of McNair Elementary School in Fort Bragg, North Carolina. She has led language arts, early childhood, and remedial reading programs for the Fort Bragg Schools, in addition to having had varied teaching experience at all levels. Ms. Brigham earned her master's degree at the University of North Carolina at Chapel Hill, where she is currently enrolled in the doctoral program in educational administration.

Teresa A. Miller has taught children in Virginia, Vermont, and North Carolina. Her degrees in education are from the College of William and Mary, and the University of North Carolina at Chapel Hill. She has worked with both children and adults in a wide variety of educational settings.

**Acknowledgements**
Cover Design: Sharon Golden, James Masch
Cover Illustration: Terrell Powell
Interior Design and Production: Dodson Publication Services
Illustrators: Peg Dougherty, Jimmy Longacre

**Staff Credits**
Executive Editor: Elizabeth Strauss
Project Editor: Chris Boyd
Project Manager: Sharon Golden

# Words with *bl-*

| bled | black | woman |
|------|-------|-------|
| block | blind | wonder |

**A.** Circle your spelling words.

1. I (wonder) where I left my books.

2. The blind man cannot see.

3. A witch hat is black.

4. A girl will grow up to be a woman.

5. They live in the same block.

6. When I cut my hand, it bled.

**B.** Circle the word that is the same as the top one.

| bled | blind | black | block | wonder | woman |
|------|-------|-------|-------|--------|-------|
| dled | blinb | blach | black | wander | wowan |
| pled | dlind | black | bluck | wouder | womar |
| (bled) | blind | block | blick | wonder | woman |
| blad | blimb | blokc | block | wonber | moman |

**C.** Find the missing letters. Then write the word.

1. b l e d _____

2. ___ ___ i n d _____

3. b l o ___ ___ _____

Name _____                    **1**

# Words with *bl-*

| bled | black | woman |
|------|-------|-------|
| block | blind | wonder |

**A.** Fill in the boxes with the right words.

1. blind

2.

3.

4.

5.

6.

**B.** Fill in each blank with the right word.

1. A girl grows up to become a **woman**.
   <br>woman   wonder

2. My foot _____ when I cut it.
   <br>block   bled

3. The _____ girl had dark hair.
   <br>blind   bled

4. Use your _____ pen.
   <br>black   block

5. I _____ if flying saucers are real.
   <br>bled   wonder

6. Do you live on the same _____ as I?
   <br>block   bled

# Words with *bl-*

| | | |
|---|---|---|
| **bled** | **black** | **woman** |
| **block** | **blind** | **wonder** |

**A.** Fill in each blank with a spelling word.

1. The ___blind___ man uses a cane.

2. Did that ___✓___ join our club?

3. Is there a new house on that _____?

**B.** Find the hidden spelling words.

```
f  o  b  l  i  n  d  z
t  l  a  r  o  p  r  b
a  w  o  m  a  n  o  l
z  o  f  t  r  n  b  e
p  n  b  u  b  k  f  d
b  d  e  b  l  o  c  k
o  e  c  r  a  l  l  d
w  r  z  y  c  a  m  h
f  t  r  n  k  b  c  e
```

**C.** Draw a line from the picture to the right word.

1.                     **a.** block

2.                     **b.** woman

Name _____

# LESSON 1

## Words with *bl-*

| bled | black | woman |
|------|-------|-------|
| block | blind | wonder |

**A.** Put an *X* on the word that is <u>not</u> the same.

| 1. | blind | blind | blind | bl~~in~~b | blind |
|----|-------|-------|-------|-------|-------|
| 2. | bled | bled | bleb | bled | bled |
| 3. | woman | woman | woman | woman | wowan |
| 4. | block | black | block | block | block |
| 5. | wonder | wonder | wonden | wonder | wonder |

**B.** Finish the sentences.

1. The <u>black</u> clouds _____.

2. The <u>woman</u> went _____.

3. I <u>wonder</u> if _____.

**C.** Use spelling words to complete the story.

Mrs. Jones is a _____ who lives on our

_____. She is a friend of our family. She is

_____.

Mrs. Jones just moved to our block. I _____

where she used to live. I bet her friends there miss her,

because she is such a nice neighbor.

4

# Words with *gl-* and *fl-*

| glad | flag | many |
|------|------|------|
| glass | flip | wash |

## A. Circle your spelling words.

1. You need to flip those pancakes.

2. Do you help wash the dishes?

3. I like to drink from a glass.

4. Are you glad that it is fall?

5. We have a flag in front of the school.

6. We can spell many new words.

## B. Circle the word that is the same as the top one.

| glad | many | glass | flag | flip | wash |
|------|------|-------|------|------|------|
| glod | mony | gloss | flag | flep | wish |
| glab | mary | glass | ftug | flop | wask |
| glad | mang | gluss | flog | flup | wash |
| glub | many | gliss | flng | flip | wosh |

## C. Find the missing letters. Then write the word.

1. _____ _____ a d          _____

2. _____ l a g          _____

3. m _____ _____ y          _____

Name _____          5

# Words with *gl-* and *fl-*

| glad | flag | many |
|------|------|------|
| glass | flip | wash |

**A.** Fill in the boxes with the right words.

1.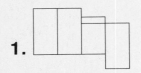

2.

3.

4.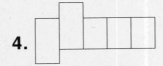

5.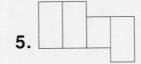

6.

**B.** Fill in each blank with the right word.

1. The American _____ is red, white, and blue.
   flip     flag

2. We do not drink from a _____ by the pool.
   glad     glass

3. I did a back _____ off the diving board.
   flip     flag

4. We _____ the car each week.
   many     wash

5. I have _____ friends at school.
   many     wash

6. I'm _____ that today is Tuesday.
   glad     glass

6

# Words with *gl-* and *fl-*

| | | |
|---|---|---|
| glad | flag | many |
| glass | flip | wash |

**A.** Use spelling words to complete the story.

I like to pretend that I live in the Wild West. I get up with the sun. I _____ pancakes over the campfire. I _____ my plate in a stream.

Then I ride my horse for _____ hours. I work with other cowboys. We take the cows up a trail. We have to watch for storms and other kinds of trouble.

At night I sleep on the ground. I like to see the stars above. I am _____ I'm a cowboy.

**B.** Finish the sentences.

1. I am <u>glad</u> when _____.

2. There are <u>many</u> _____.

3. The <u>flag</u> almost _____.

**C.** Write words that begin like each word below.

| <u>gl</u>ad | <u>fl</u>ag | <u>m</u>any | <u>w</u>ash |
|---|---|---|---|
| glue | _____ | _____ | _____ |
| _____ | _____ | _____ | _____ |

Name _____

7

# LESSON 2

## Words with *gl-* and *fl-*

| glad | flag | many |
|------|------|------|
| glass | flip | wash |

**A.** Write each word three times.

1. flag  _____  _____  _____

2. wash  _____  _____  _____

3. glad  _____  _____  _____

4. many  _____  _____  _____

5. glass  _____  _____  _____

6. flip  _____  _____  _____

**B.** Draw a line from the word to the right picture.

1. flip                                    a.

2. glass                                   b.

3. flag                                    c.

**C.** Put an *X* on the word that is <u>not</u> the same.

| 1. wash | wash | wask | wash | wash |
|---------|------|------|------|------|
| 2. flip | fliq | flip | flip | flip |
| 3. glad | glad | glad | glad | glab |

8

# Words with *pl-* and *sl-*

| | | |
|---|---|---|
| plant | slept | small |
| plus | slid | try |

**A.** Circle your spelling words.

1. Our car slid on the ice.

2. My sock has a small hole in it.

3. Two plus two is four.

4. We went to a plant store.

5. I will try to be a better friend.

6. We slept in a tent at camp.

**B.** Find the missing letters. Then write the word.

1. p l _____ _____ _____      _____

2. _____ _____ e p t          _____

3. _____ m _____ _____ l      _____

**C.** Use spelling words to complete the story.

Last winter my family was driving across town. It was snowing. The car _____ on ice. We went off the side of the road. The car landed in a _____ ditch. We were frightened. But a tow truck pulled us out of the ditch.

Name _____

9

# Words with *pl-* and *sl-*

| plant | slept | small |
|-------|-------|-------|
| plus  | slid  | try   |

**A.** Circle the word that is the same as the top one.

| plant | plus | try | slept | slid | small |
|-------|------|-----|-------|------|-------|
| dlant | blus | fry | slipt | sled | smell |
| plant | dlus | tny | slopt | slud | snell |
| olant | plus | trv | slupt | slod | small |
| ptant | plos | try | slept | slid | swall |

**B.** Fill in each blank with the right word.

1. Seven _____ seven is fourteen.
   plant    plus

2. I _____ across the wet floor.
   slid    slept

3. You cannot do it unless you _____.
   try    small

4. Eat a _____ bit of each food on
   try    small

your tray.

5. A corn _____ is tall.
   plus    plant

# Words with *pl-* and *sl-*

| plant | slept | small |
|-------|-------|-------|
| plus | slid | try |

**A.** Fill in the boxes with the right words.

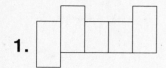  1.

  2.

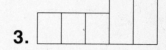  3.

  4.

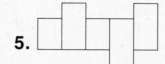  5.

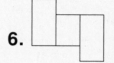  6.

**B.** Write the spelling words in ABC order.

1. __plant__    2. __plus__    3. _____

4. _____    5. _____    6. _____

**C.** Find the hidden spelling words.

```
e  n  o  g  s  r  v  x  t  w
v  a  b  p  l  a  n  t  i  n
e  i  p  r  e  g  r  o  w  l
p  l  u  s  p  x  t  l  a  b
f  l  i  r  t  s  s  l  i  d
b  c  d  t  f  m  g  h  j  k
l  m  n  r  p  a  q  r  s  t
v  w  a  y  e  l  i  o  u  y
r  b  i  t  d  l  p  a  t  g
```

Name _____

# Words with *pl-* and *sl-*

| plant | slept | small |
|-------|-------|-------|
| plus  | slid  | try   |

**A.** Put an *X* on the word that is <u>not</u> the same.

| | | | | |
|---|---|---|---|---|
| **1.** slept | slept | slept | slcpt | slept |
| **2.** try | try | tny | try | try |
| **3.** slid | slib | slid | slid | slid |
| **4.** plant | plant | plant | plant | plart |
| **5.** small | snall | small | small | small |
| **6.** plus | plns | plus | plus | plus |

**B.** Finish the sentences.

1. I <u>slept</u> until _____.

2. The box <u>slid</u> _____.

**C.** Write each word three times.

1. slept _____ _____ _____

2. small _____ _____ _____

3. plus _____ _____ _____

4. try _____ _____ _____

5. slid _____ _____ _____

6. plant _____ _____ _____

# Words with *sc-* and *scr-*

| scalp | scrub | plenty |
|-------|----------|--------|
| scan | scribble | brown |

## A. Circle your spelling words.

1. Please scrub the tub after your bath.

2. Do you have brown hair?

3. Your hair grows from your scalp.

4. We have plenty of food in the house.

5. Scan the page for the answer to my question.

6. You scribble when you write too fast.

## B. Find the missing letters. Then write the word.

1. s c _____ _____ _____ b l e    _____

2. _____ _____ a l p    _____

3. _____ _____ _____ u b    _____

## C. Circle the word that is the same as the top one.

| scalp | brown | scan | plenty | scribble | scrub |
|-------|-------|------|--------|----------|-------|
| scald | brawn | scan | planty | scriddle | scrud |
| scalb | brown | scar | plemty | scribdle | serub |
| scalp | bnown | sear | plenyt | scribble | scnub |
| sealp | bromn | scon | plenty | scnibble | scrub |

Name _____

# Words with *sc-* and *scr-*

| scalp | scrub | plenty |
|-------|-------|--------|
| scan | scribble | brown |

**A.** Find the hidden spelling words.

```
n w o z f t u g a l
t r m s c a l p s s
b s c a n m n g h f
s c r i b b l e r n
c r p q p r f g p v
p u r s l o z w n g
u b t u e w p r s g
b l c n n n i n g o
r r v p t n f r o p
s a l p y r f g p v
f m n g h o z w n g
```

**B.** Fill in each blank with a spelling word.

1. _____ the page for the right answer.

2. I can't read your writing when you _____.

3. You must _____ the floor to clean it.

**C.** Write the spelling words in ABC order.

1. _____    2. _____    3. _____

4. _____    5. _____    6. _____

14

# Words with *sc-* and *scr-*

| | | |
|---|---|---|
| scalp | scrub | plenty |
| scan | scribble | brown |

**A.** Fill in each blank with the right word.

1. Do you _____ the sink after you wash dishes?
   scalp   scrub

2. Dirt is often the color _____.
   scan   brown

3. Use your best handwriting. Do not _____.
   scribble   scalp

4. I like _____ of cheese on pizza.
   plenty   scan

5. Your _____ gets itchy when your hair is not clean.
   scribble   scalp

**B.** Write the spelling words that rhyme with the words below.

1. down     gown     frown     _____

2. sub     cub     tub     _____

3. man     ran     can     _____

**C.** Write these words from lessons before.

1. many _____     2. flag _____

3. wash _____     4. plus _____

Name _____

# Words with *sc-* and *scr-*

| scalp | scrub | plenty |
|-------|-------|--------|
| scan | scribble | brown |

**A.** Put an *X* on the word that is <u>not</u> the same.

| 1. | scribble | scribble | seribble | scribble | scribble |
|----|----------|----------|----------|----------|----------|
| 2. | plenty | plenty | plenty | planty | plenty |
| 3. | scan | scar | scan | scan | scan |
| 4. | scrub | scrub | scrub | scrud | scrub |
| 5. | scalp | scalp | scalp | scalp | scolp |
| 6. | brown | brown | broun | brown | brown |

**B.** Finish the sentences.

1. I like to <u>scribble</u> on _____.

2. I <u>scan</u> the newspaper for _____.

**C.** Use spelling words to complete the story.

Everyone should know how to make mud pies. Fill a pan

or bucket with _____ of good dirt. Next, add water

to the dirt, until it becomes a nice _____ dough. It

will feel good to squish the mud through your fingers.

After that, pat out the pies and put them in a sunny place.

Go _____ your hands and wait for the pies to bake.

| skill | snap | flute |
|-------|------|-------|
| skunk | snack | goes |

**A.** Circle your spelling words.

1. A skunk is a black and white animal.

2. Can you play the flute?

3. Do you know how to snap your fingers?

4. A plane goes fast.

5. Do you eat a snack before going to bed?

6. It takes a lot of skill to play basketball well.

**B.** Use spelling words to complete the story.

The girl wanted to learn a new _____.

"I think I'll learn how to play the _____," she said.

She bought a flute. She bought a book for beginners. She

thought it would be a _____.

But it wasn't. She had trouble learning the notes in the book.

Maybe I should take lessons, she thought. The girl found a

teacher. Soon she became very good at playing the flute.

**C.** Write the spelling word that rhymes with the words below.

crack    back    _____

Name_____

# LESSON 5

## Words with *sk-* and *sn-*

| | | |
|---|---|---|
| skill | snap | flute |
| skunk | snack | goes |

**A.** Fill in each blank with the right word.

1. Can you _____ your fingers?
   <small>snap    snack</small>

2. That animal is a _____.
   <small>skill    skunk</small>

3. It takes _____ to do well at any sport.
   <small>skill    skunk</small>

4. I love to play the _____.
   <small>goes    flute</small>

5. The road _____ to the lake.
   <small>snap    goes</small>

6. Do you eat a _____ between meals?
   <small>snack    snap</small>

**B.** Find the missing letters. Then write the word.

_____ _____ i l l          _____

**C.** Write the spelling words in ABC order.

1. _____   2. _____   3. _____

4. _____   5. _____   6. _____

18

| skill | snap | flute |
|-------|------|-------|
| skunk | snack | goes |

## A. Fill in the boxes with the right words.

1.

2.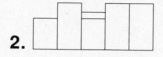

3.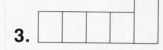

4.

5.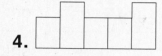

6.

## B. Fill in each blank with a spelling word.

1. It takes _____ to sing well.

2. The _____ smells bad.

3. Would you like a _____ to eat?

## C. Draw a line from the word to the right picture.

1. snack          a.

2. flute          b.

3. snap           c.

Name _____

# Words with *sk-* and *sn-*

| skill | snap | flute |
|-------|-------|-------|
| skunk | snack | goes |

**A.** Put an *X* on the word that is <u>not</u> the same.

| 1. | flute | flute | flute | fluet | flute |
|----|-------|-------|-------|-------|-------|
| 2. | snack | snake | snack | snack | snack |
| 3. | skill | shill | skill | skill | skill |
| 4. | goes | goes | goes | goes | gose |
| 5. | snap | snap | snop | snap | snap |
| 6. | skunk | skunk | skunk | sknuk | skunk |

**B.** Finish the sentences.

1. The <u>skunk</u> _____.

2. My favorite <u>snack</u> is _____.

**C.** Write each word three times.

1. flute _____ _____ _____

2. snack _____ _____ _____

3. skill _____ _____ _____

4. snap _____ _____ _____

5. goes _____ _____ _____

6. skunk _____ _____ _____

# Words with *sp-* and *st-*

| spend | study | never |
|-------|-------|-------|
| spill | stamp | warm |

## A. Circle your spelling words.

1. Do not forget to study your spelling.

2. Never go for a ride with someone you don't know.

3. I do not have any money to spend.

4. Soon you will have to pay more for a stamp.

5. Be careful not to spill your tea.

6. I wear warm clothes on cold days.

## B. Use spelling words to complete the story.

Let's try to _____ fifteen minutes each night

working on spelling words. We'll work at our desks.

We can _____ best in our own rooms. We should

_____ work in front of the TV.

## C. Write these words from lessons before.

1. scrub _____

2. black _____

3. scribble _____

4. snap _____

5. snack _____

6. skunk _____

7. scalp _____

8. brown _____

Name _____

# Words with *sp-* and *st-*

| spend | study | never |
|-------|-------|-------|
| spill | stamp | warm |

## A. Fill in each blank with the right word.

1. How do you _____ your spelling words?
   <br>stamp    study

2. When you fill the car with gas, try not to _____
   <br>spend   spill
   <br>any.

3. I hope you _____ eat seven hot dogs again.
   <br>never   spend

4. If you don't _____ all your money, you can save some.
   <br>spend   warm

5. We like to play outdoors on _____ days.
   <br>warm   stamp

## B. Find the hidden spelling words.

```
y  d  s  t  u  d  y  r
q  i  p  m  a  g  r  o
s  d  i  z  r  o  o  b
m  w  l  s  p  e  n  d
f  a  l  t  p  q  e  e
g  r  b  a  r  b  v  r
l  m  q  m  o  c  e  j
h  i  f  p  p  d  r  z
```

# Words with *sp-* and *st-*

| spend | study | never |
|-------|-------|-------|
| spill | stamp | warm |

**A.** Find the missing letters. Then write the word.

1. _____ _____ e n d _____

2. s p _____ _____ _____ _____

**B.** Write the spelling words in ABC order.

1. _____  2. _____  3. _____

4. _____  5. _____  6. _____

**C.** Write words that begin like each word below.

spend        stamp        never        warm

_____     _____     _____     _____

_____     _____     _____     _____

**D.** Fill in the boxes with the right words.

1. 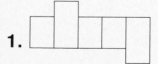     2.      3.

4.                5.                6.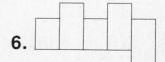

Name _____

# Words with *sp-* and *st-*

| spend | study | never |
|-------|-------|-------|
| spill | stamp | warm |

## A. Finish the sentences.

1. Sometimes I <u>spill</u> _____.

2. It is <u>warm</u> _____.

3. I like to <u>spend</u> my time _____.

## B. Circle the word that is the same as the top one.

| <u>stamp</u> | <u>warm</u> | <u>study</u> | <u>spend</u> | <u>never</u> | <u>spill</u> |
|-------|------|-------|-------|-------|-------|
| stump | warw | stady | spend | rever | spell |
| stawp | marm | stuyd | sperd | never | sqill |
| stamp | worm | study | spenb | newer | sgill |
| sfump | warm | sludy | speud | neven | spill |

## C. Write each word three times.

1. spill _____ _____ _____

2. never _____ _____ _____

3. stamp _____ _____ _____

4. study _____ _____ _____

5. spend _____ _____ _____

6. warm _____ _____ _____

| swing | swimming | book |
|-------|----------|------|
| swim | arm | four |

**A.  Circle your spelling words.**

1. Monkeys like to swing from tree to tree.

2. This book will teach me many new words.

3. Two plus two is four.

4. Do you know how to swim?

5. I broke my arm when I fell.

6. Swimming is fun.

**B.  Write the spelling words that rhyme with the words below.**

1. sing    thing    _____

2. farm    harm    _____

3. look    took    _____

4. dim    rim    _____

**C.  Use spelling words to complete the story.**

The twins had a fun summer. On their birthday in June,

they got a _____ set. It was put in their backyard.

They spent almost every day _____ in their friend's

pool. In July, they spent _____ weeks on a farm.

Name _____    25

# Words with *sw-*

| swing | swimming | book |
|-------|----------|------|
| swim | arm | four |

**A.** Fill in each blank with the right word.

1. Let's go _____ at the pool.
   <u>arm    swimming</u>

2. I want to check out a _____ about jets.
   <u>swim    book</u>

3. It's fun to _____ in the summertime.
   <u>swim    book</u>

4. We vote for a president every _____ years.
   <u>book    four</u>

5. My sister broke her _____.
   <u>arm    swimming</u>

6. My dad made a _____ to play on.
   <u>swing    book</u>

**B.** Write the spelling words in ABC order.

1. _____    2. _____    3. _____

4. _____    5. _____    6. _____

**C.** Fill in the blank with a spelling word.

I went for a _____ with my brother.

# LESSON 7    Words with *sw-*

| swing | swimming | book |
|-------|----------|------|
| swim  | arm      | four |

**A.** Find the hidden spelling words.

```
p  s  e  r  n  a  g  z  a
s  w  i  n  g  b  o  o  k
w  i  a  t  r  f  o  o  o
i  m  a  v  m  g  d  t  m
m  m  f  o  u  r  r  z  k
u  i  i  e  f  z  n  c  t
o  n  b  e  a  b  o  u  t
i  g  e  n  a  r  m  s  o
```

**B.** Fill in the boxes with the right words.

1.

2. 

3.

4. 

5. 

6. 

**C.** Write these words from lessons before.

1. woman _____
2. glass _____
3. plant _____
4. scalp _____
5. snack _____
6. study _____

Name _____

27

# Words with *sw-*

| swing | swimming | book |
|-------|----------|------|
| swim | arm | four |

## A. Write each word three times.

1. swim      _____    _____    _____

2. swimming    _____    _____    _____

3. swing      _____    _____    _____

4. arm       _____    _____    _____

5. four       _____    _____    _____

6. book      _____    _____    _____

## B. Circle the word that is the same as the top one.

| arm | book | swim | swimming | four | swing |
|-----|------|------|----------|------|-------|
| ram | booh | swin | smimming | foun | swing |
| amr | dook | swim | snimming | tour | swirg |
| mar | book | smim | swimming | fonr | swinq |
| arm | boak | swiw | swimmimg | four | sming |

## C. Finish the sentences.

1. Your <u>arm</u> is _____.

2. A <u>book</u> is _____.

3. I can eat <u>four</u> _____.

28

# Words with *cr-*

| crust | crash | much |
|-------|-------|------|
| crack | myself | kind |

**A.** Circle your spelling words.

1. Two cars were in a crash.

2. The boy was kind to his dog.

3. I try to do something nice for myself each day.

4. The crust on this pie tastes good.

5. I do not like liver very much.

6. There is a crack in the mirror.

**B.** Use spelling words to complete the story.

Last week my aunt was going to the store in her new car. Something she didn't expect happened. Her car was in a

_____.

A truck ran a red light and hit the new car. My aunt is all right. But there's a big _____ in the window, and the bumper is badly bent.

My aunt wonders how _____ it will cost to fix her car. She hopes that her car will look as good as new when it comes back from the shop.

Name _____

# Words with *cr-*

| | | |
|---|---|---|
| crust | crash | much |
| crack | myself | kind |

**A.** Fill in each blank with the right word.

1. I bought the apple _____.
   myself    much

2. She made a pie with a beautiful _____.
   crust    crack

3. A rock hit the window and made a _____ in it.
   crust    crack

4. The car and truck were in a _____.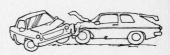
   crack    crash

**B.** Write the spelling words in ABC order.

1. _____    2. _____    3. _____

4. _____    5. _____    6. _____

**C.** Find the hidden spelling words.

```
f  m  a  b  b  k  i  n  g  h
m  u  f  b  r  i  n  g  e  c
p  c  f  s  i  n  r  o  v  r
a  h  g  h  c  d  j  o  k  a
c  r  a  c  k  o  o  d  a  s
p  r  c  r  u  s  t  o  s  h
z  o  m  y  s  e  l  f  b  s
```

# Words with *cr-*

| crust | crash | much |
|-------|-------|------|
| crack | myself | kind |

## A. Fill in the boxes with the right words.

1.

2.

3.

4.

5.

6.

## B. Find the missing letters. Then write the word.

1. m _____ _____ h          _____

2. m y _____ _____ _____ _____          _____

3. _____ _____ u s t          _____

## C. Circle the word that is the same as the top one.

| crust | crash | much | crack | kind | myself |
|-------|-------|------|-------|------|--------|
| crusf | crush | nuch | crack | kird | myselt |
| cnust | crash | muck | cnack | kirb | mvself |
| crost | crask | much | cvack | kind | mgself |
| crust | crahs | mnck | crach | kinb | myself |

Name _____

# Words with *cr-*

| crust | crash | much |
|-------|--------|------|
| crack | myself | kind |

**A.** Draw a line from the word to the right picture.

1. crust

2. crash

3. crack

**B.** Finish the sentences.

1. I like <u>myself</u> when _____ .

2. Be <u>kind</u> _____ .

**C.** Write each word three times.

1. myself _____ _____ _____

2. kind _____ _____ _____

3. much _____ _____ _____

4. crash _____ _____ _____

5. crack _____ _____ _____

6. crust _____ _____ _____

# Words with *dr-* and *gr-*

| | | |
|---|---|---|
| drum | grass | frog |
| drink | grab | done |

## A. Circle your spelling words.

1. Milk is a good drink.

2. That frog makes funny noises at night.

3. How much work have you done?

4. Many bands have a bass drum.

5. A robber may try to grab your purse.

6. In the winter the grass turns brown.

## B. Use spelling words to complete the story.

One sunny afternoon, my friend and I took a picnic lunch

down by the lake. We sat on a dock near some tall

_____. While we talked, we ate our peanut butter

crackers and drank tea.

Loud sounds came from the tall grass. We wondered what

had made the noise. Then we saw a frog. I wanted to keep

the _____ for a pet, so I tried to _____ its

leg. But the frog hopped away. We never saw it again, but

we still go to the lake to look for it.

Name _____

# Words with *dr-* and *gr-*

| drum | grass | frog |
|------|-------|------|
| drink | grab | done |

**A.** Fill in each blank with the right word.

1. Do you like to _____ milk?
   <sub>grab    drink</sub>

2. I like to hear _____ noises at night.
   <sub>grass    frog</sub>

3. What kind of _____ would you like to play?
   <sub>drum    done</sub>

4. I cut the _____ in my yard.
   <sub>drink    grass</sub>

5. Have you _____ something nice for someone today?
   <sub>drum    done</sub>

6. Please do not _____ the papers from my hand.
   <sub>grab    drink</sub>

**B.** Find the hidden spelling words.

```
d  z  f  g  r  a  s  s
o  d  r  i  n  k  p  o
n  r  o  g  h  h  r  d
e  u  g  r  e  a  f  l
n  m  i  a  p  v  n  v
p  r  p  b  e  e  o  e
```

# Words with *dr-* and *gr-*

| drum | grass | frog |
|------|-------|------|
| drink | grab | done |

**A.** Find the missing letters. Then write the word.

1. _____ _____ u m      _____

2. _____ _____ o g      _____

3. d _____ n _____      _____

**B.** Write the spelling words in ABC order.

1. _____   2. _____   3. _____

4. _____   5. _____   6. _____

**C.** Circle the word that is the same as the top one.

| grab | drum | done | grass | frog | drink |
|------|------|------|-------|------|-------|
| qrab | brum | bone | grass | trog | drinh |
| grad | druw | dore | qrass | frog | drirk |
| grab | drnm | done | gnass | froq | brink |
| gnab | drum | donc | graas | frug | drink |

**D.** Finish the sentences.

1. I put a frog _____.

2. Don't grab the _____.

Name _____

35

# Words with *dr-* and *gr-*

| | | |
|---|---|---|
| drum | grass | frog |
| drink | grab | done |

## A. Draw a line from the picture to the right word.

1.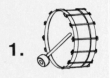

**a.** drink

2.

**b.** frog

3.

**c.** drum

## B. Fill in the boxes with the right words.

1. 

2. 

3. 

4. 

5. 

6. 

## C. Write each word three times.

1. drink  _____  _____  _____

2. grass  _____  _____  _____

3. frog  _____  _____  _____

4. done  _____  _____  _____

5. grab  _____  _____  _____

# Words with *pr-* and *str-*

| prompt | string | group |
|--------|--------|-------|
| press | strap | laugh |

**A.** Circle your spelling words.

1. You use an iron to press your clothes.

2. We flew a kite on a long string.

3. We will stay with our group on the field trip.

4. If you are on time, you are prompt.

5. A good teacher knows how to laugh.

6. My purse has a strap to hold on to.

**B.** Write the spelling words that rhyme with the words below.

1. mess     dress     _____

2. wing     sing     _____

3. lap     nap     _____

**C.** Finish the sentences.

1. I like to <u>laugh</u> at _____ .

2. I use a <u>string</u> _____ .

**D.** Find the missing letters. Then write the word.

1. ____ ____ o m ____ t     _____

2. ____ ____ ____ g h     _____

Name _____

# Words with *pr-* and *str-*

| prompt | string | group |
|--------|--------|-------|
| press | strap | laugh |

**A.** Fill in each blank with the right word.

1. Fly the kite on a _____.
   string   strap

2. They are in my reading _____.
   group   press

3. Use an iron to _____ the clothes.
   group   press

4. My purse has a shoulder _____.
   string   strap

5. You are a _____ person if you are on time.
   prompt   laugh

**B.** Write words that begin like each word below.

g̲roup        p̲ress        st̲ring        l̲augh

_____    _____    _____    _____

_____    _____    _____    _____

**C.** Write the spelling words in ABC order.

1. _____    2. _____    3. _____

4. _____    5. _____    6. _____

# Words with *pr-* and *str-*

| prompt | string | group |
|--------|--------|-------|
| press  | strap  | laugh |

**A.** Use spelling words to complete the story.

Next weekend, our scout troop will go to the beach. We plan to fly kites all day. We need to be _____ and get to school by 8:00 A.M., so that we can leave by 8:15. Someone will need to bring extra _____. Last year we didn't have enough!

There's not a place to buy food or drinks at the beach, so we can't forget to bring our lunches. Let's be ready so our _____ can have lots of fun!

**B.** Write each word two times in cursive.

*laugh* _____

*press* _____

*string* _____

*strap* _____

*group* _____

*prompt* _____

**C.** Which spelling word ends with an *f* sound? _____

© 1991 Steck-Vaughn Company. Target 360

Name _____

**39**

# LESSON 10 — Words with *pr-* and *str-*

| prompt | string | group |
|--------|--------|-------|
| press | strap | laugh |

**A.** Fill in the boxes with the right words.

1. 2. 3.

4. 5. 6.

**B.** Write these words from lessons before.

1. crust _____    2. myself _____

3. crack _____    4. drum _____

5. frog _____    6. drink _____

**C.** Write each word three times.

1. strap _____ _____ _____

2. laugh _____ _____ _____

3. press _____ _____ _____

4. group _____ _____ _____

5. string _____ _____ _____

6. prompt _____ _____ _____

# Words with *tr-* and *cl-*

| | | |
|---|---|---|
| trip | club | again |
| trust | class | after |

**A.** Circle your spelling words.

1. Do you belong to the stamp club?

2. Our group took a field trip to a dairy.

3. "In God We Trust" is written on a penny.

4. You are not in my class at school.

5. Will you take me for a plane ride again?

6. We will leave for the store after lunch.

**B.** Use spelling words to complete the story.

_____ lunch on Friday, our _____ will

visit the zoo. We plan to go by bus. We'll sing songs and

play games on the _____. We hope to see snakes,

bears, and lions. I hear they have a monkey island. It will

really be fun!

**C.** Write the spelling words in ABC order.

1. _____   2. _____   3. _____

4. _____   5. _____   6. _____

Name _____

# Words with *tr-* and *cl-*

| trip | club | again |
|------|------|-------|
| trust | class | after |

**A.** Fill in each blank with the right word.

1. Boy Scouts is a _____.
   <br>trust    club

2. I _____ you to do the right thing.
   <br>trust    trip

3. How many girls are in our _____?
   <br>class    trip

4. Please sing each line _____ me.
   <br>again    after

5. Let's sing the song _____.
   <br>again    after

6. Our family goes on a _____ together during the summer.
   <br>trust    trip

**B.** Write the spelling words that rhyme with the words below.

1. lip       rip       _____

2. rub       tub       _____

3. dust      rust      _____

4. grass     pass      _____

5. rafter    laughter  _____

42

| trip | club | again |
|------|------|-------|
| trust | class | after |

**A.** Find the hidden spelling words.

```
r s o m e b o d y e s
a f m u a t r i p o p
f a n p g r o c a c e
t t o o a u d a r l d
e e n p i s e a t a o
r i r e n t a o y s e
g s c l u b o o p s t
o f a m i l y s s e a
```

**B.** Find the missing letters. Then write the word.

c _____ _____ s _____        _____

**C.** Write each word three times.

**1.** club      _____  _____  _____

**2.** class     _____  _____  _____

**3.** trip      _____  _____  _____

**4.** trust     _____  _____  _____

**5.** again     _____  _____  _____

**6.** after     _____  _____  _____

© 1991 Steck-Vaughn Company. Target 360

# Words with *tr-* and *cl-*

| trip | club | again |
|------|------|-------|
| trust | class | after |

**A.** Put an *X* on the word that is <u>not</u> the same.

| | | | | |
|---|---|---|---|---|
| **1.** trip | trip | trip | trap | trip |
| **2.** club | club | clab | club | club |
| **3.** trust | trusf | trust | trust | trust |
| **4.** class | class | class | class | calss |
| **5.** again | again | again | aigan | again |
| **6.** after | after | atfer | after | after |

**B.** Write each word two times in cursive.

*club*

*class*

*after*

*again*

*trip*

*trust*

**C.** Which spelling word has three vowels? _____

# Words with *-ank, -unk,* and *-nch*

| drank | trunk | inch |
|-------|-------|------|
| bank | junk | pinch |

## A. Circle your spelling words.

1. I drank three glasses of milk yesterday.

2. The dart missed the balloon by an inch.

3. I put my money in the bank.

4. We keep winter clothes in a trunk in the summer.

5. It hurts when you pinch me.

6. This room is full of junk.

## B. Fill in each blank with the right word.

1. The recipe called for a _____ of salt.
   <br>trunk   pinch

2. If you save all that _____, you'll have to throw it away later.
   <br>inch   junk

3. The safest place for your money is the _____.
   <br>bank   pinch

4. The fuse on this firecracker is an _____ long.
   <br>inch   pinch

5. An elephant has a long _____.
   <br>drank   trunk

6. The big dog _____ all the water.
   <br>drank   bank

Name _____

# Words with *-ank, -unk,* and *-nch*

| drank | trunk | inch |
|-------|-------|------|
| bank  | junk  | pinch |

**A.** Write the spelling words in ABC order.

1. _____  2. _____  3. _____

4. _____  5. _____  6. _____

**B.** Use spelling words to complete the story.

I bought a used car last week. After I drove it home, I

looked in the _____. It was full of _____!

There wasn't an _____ of space left in it. I guess I'll

have to clean it all out. Maybe I'll find a buried treasure in all

that junk.

**C.** Find the hidden spelling words.

```
n b c r e e l s o j
a b c t u b a y s u
w b c p b a d o w n
p r o s a t r u n k
i n c h a s a n a p
n b c a s k n o w m
c a r b a n k n e e
h z q e y u i s e e
r t v e s t d f o r
```

# Words with -ank, -unk, and -nch

| drank | trunk | inch |
|-------|-------|------|
| bank | junk | pinch |

**A.** Write the spelling words that rhyme with the words below.

1. finch    inch    _____

2. hunk    junk    _____

3. bank    rank    _____

**B.** Find the missing letters. Then write the word.

1. _____ _____ c h    _____

2. _____ _____ u n k    _____

**C.** Write each word two times in cursive.

*bank* _____

*drank* _____

*trunk* _____

*junk* _____

*inch* _____

*pinch* _____

**D.** Which spelling word begins with a vowel? _____

Name _____

# Words with *-ank*, *-unk*, and *-nch*

| drank | trunk | inch |
|-------|-------|------|
| bank | junk | pinch |

**A.** Write each word three times.

1. inch _____ _____ _____

2. pinch _____ _____ _____

3. drank _____ _____ _____

4. bank _____ _____ _____

5. trunk _____ _____ _____

6. junk _____ _____ _____

**B.** Circle the word that is the same as the top one.

| inch | drank | bank | pinch | trunk | junk |
|------|-------|------|-------|-------|------|
| inck | brank | dank | piuch | trank | jank |
| irch | drink | bank | pinck | trink | jonk |
| inch | drunk | dunk | pinch | trnnk | junk |
| iuch | drank | bunk | pirch | trunk | jnnk |

**C.** Fill in the boxes with the right words.

1.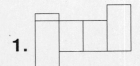

2.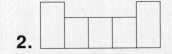

3.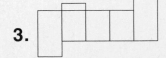

# Words with -*anch* and -*ung*

| branch | swung | together |
|--------|-------|----------|
| ranch | strung | today |

## A. Circle your spelling words.

1. We strung some beads to make a necklace.

2. Cows and horses live on a ranch.

3. Our family was together for the holiday.

4. The monkey swung from a tree.

5. I broke a branch off the tree.

6. What are we having for lunch today?

## B. Fill in each blank with the right word.

1. We _____ a clothesline from the house to the garage.
   <u>ranch    strung</u>

2. I rode a horse on the _____.
   <u>branch    ranch</u>

3. Let's do our homework _____ instead of tomorrow.
   <u>together    today</u>

4. I like to put model planes _____.
   <u>together    today</u>

5. The door _____ open in the strong wind.
   <u>swung    ranch</u>

6. The wind blew the _____ off the tree.
   <u>branch    strung</u>

Name _____

# Words with *-anch* and *-ung*

| branch | swung | together |
|--------|--------|----------|
| ranch | strung | today |

**A.** Write words that end like each word below.

swu<u>ng</u>  to<u>day</u>  ran<u>ch</u>

_____  _____  _____

_____  _____  _____

**B.** Use spelling words to complete the story.

I went to the park _____ with my best friend. We had a great time.

First, we _____ on the swings and went down the slide. Then we saw a big tree _____ lying across the creek. We walked across the branch. Then we got brave and walked backward. We began to laugh, and I fell in the creek! The water wasn't deep, though. My friend laughed so hard he nearly fell, too. We always have fun _____.

**C.** Write these words from lessons before.

1. trust _____  2. again _____

3. inch _____  4. drank _____

5. junk _____  6. pinch _____

# Words with *-anch* and *-ung*

| | | |
|---|---|---|
| **branch** | **swung** | **together** |
| **ranch** | **strung** | **today** |

**A.** Write words that begin like each word below.

<u>sw</u>ung      <u>str</u>ung      <u>br</u>anch      <u>r</u>anch

_____    _____    _____    _____

_____    _____    _____    _____

_____    _____    _____    _____

**B.** Find the missing letters. Then write the word.

1. _____ _____ _____ c h      _____

2. s w _____ _____ _____      _____

3. b r _____ _____ _____ h      _____

**C.** Write each word three times.

1. branch _____    _____    _____

2. ranch _____    _____    _____

3. swung _____    _____    _____

4. strung _____    _____    _____

5. together _____    _____    _____

6. today _____    _____    _____

Name _____

# Words with *-anch* and *-ung*

| branch | swung | together |
|--------|-------|----------|
| ranch | strung | today |

**A.** Write each word two times in cursive.

*together*

*swung*

*strung*

*today*

*ranch*

*branch*

**B.** Circle the word that is the same as the top one.

| branch | ranch | swung | strung | today | together |
|--------|-------|-------|--------|-------|----------|
| brunch | ranch | smung | stnung | tobay | toqrther |
| bnarch | rench | swnng | strumg | foday | together |
| branch | ranck | swuug | stnnng | todag | togefher |
| brank | rauch | swung | strung | today | togethen |

**C.** Finish the sentences.

1. The <u>ranch</u> is _____.

2. <u>Today</u> I'm going to _____.

52

| wink | collar | full |
|------|--------|------|
| blink | dollar | hurt |

## A. Circle your spelling words.

1. How many times each minute do your eyes blink?

2. The basket was full of clothes.

3. The dog has a collar.

4. The candy costs a dollar.

5. If I wink, you'll know that I'm playing a trick.

6. The fox was hurt by the trap.

## B. Fill in each blank with the right word.

1. Can you _____ with just one eye?
   full    wink

2. The dog's _____ is too big.
   dollar    collar

3. Does a pie cost more than a _____?
   full    dollar

4. When your eyes are tired, they sometimes _____.
   blink    dollar

5. Her plate was _____ of good things to eat.
   hurt    full

6. The cut on my hand does not _____ now.
   hurt    full

Name _____    53

# Words with *-ink* and *-ar*

| | | |
|---|---|---|
| wink | collar | full |
| blink | dollar | hurt |

## A. Find the hidden spelling words.

```
s  d  o  r  e  b  y  b  f  d  c  p
l  o  m  o  v  s  m  f  u  m  o  r
e  l  a  w  i  n  k  a  l  l  l  x
e  l  k  i  b  g  e  v  l  u  l  n
p  a  a  n  l  i  y  a  m  s  a  o
h  r  n  g  i  n  g  y  h  u  r  t
o  p  d  o  n  g  u  m  e  w  f  i
r  l  s  e  k  r  e  a  r  e  t  p
```

## B. Fill in the boxes with the right words.

1.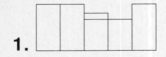

2.

3.

4.

5.

6.

## C. Write these words from lessons before.

1. trust _____

2. class _____

3. drank _____

4. pinch _____

# Words with *-ink* and *-ar*

| wink | collar | full |
|------|--------|------|
| blink | dollar | hurt |

**A.** Use spelling words to complete the story.

My dog Wags was almost run over. He ran across the street in front of our house. Wags was tied to a tree, but he slipped out of his _____. Then he ran toward the street.

Our street is usually _____ of cars, but only one was coming this time. The driver saw Wags and turned the wheel to keep from hitting him. I was so happy that Wags was not _____!

**B.** Find the missing letters. Then write the word.

f _____ _____ _____          _____

**C.** Write each word three times.

**1.** blink      _____  _____  _____

**2.** collar     _____  _____  _____

**3.** full       _____  _____  _____

**4.** hurt       _____  _____  _____

**5.** wink       _____  _____  _____

**6.** dollar     _____  _____  _____

Name _____

# Words with *-ink* and *-ar*

| wink | collar | full |
|------|--------|------|
| blink | dollar | hurt |

**A.** Write each word two times in cursive.

*wink* _____

*full* _____

*collar* _____

*dollar* _____

*hurt* _____

*blink* _____

**B.** Circle the word that is the same as the top one.

| collar | wink | hurt | full | dollar | blink |
|--------|------|------|------|--------|-------|
| collur | winh | burt | tull | dollar | blinh |
| coller | wirk | hunt | full | doller | dlink |
| coler | wink | hurt | fnll | dallor | blink |
| collar | wiuk | bunt | foll | dollur | blirk |

**C.** Finish the sentences.

1. It can <u>hurt</u> when _____.

2. I paid a <u>dollar</u> for _____.

56

# Words with *th-*

| these | think | pretty |
|-------|-------|--------|
| those | thank | eight |

## A. Circle your spelling words.

1. Thank you for the gift.

2. You look pretty in your new dress.

3. Please hand me those papers.

4. How old do you think I am?

5. Eight eggs are left.

6. I like these jeans on the rack next to me.

## B. Fill in each blank with the right word.

1. I want one of _____ apples over there.
   <br>these    those

2. _____ girls went swimming.
   <br>Eight    Think

3. Who do you _____ will win the game?
   <br>thank    think

4. I want to _____ you for the gift.
   <br>thank    think

5. May I give you one of _____ flowers?
   <br>these    pretty

6. How _____ you look!
   <br>these    pretty

Name _____

# Words with *th-*

| | | |
|---|---|---|
| these | think | pretty |
| those | thank | eight |

**A.** Write the spelling words in ABC order.

1. _____   2. _____   3. _____

4. _____   5. _____   6. _____

**B.** Find the hidden spelling words.

```
a  u  a  d  l  a  o  n  e
i  t  s  b  e  a  r  t  o
t  h  e  s  e  r  e  h  e
a  e  a  l  l  a  r  o  t
e  i  g  h  t  e  s  s  h
l  v  i  e  o  v  u  e  i
p  r  e  t  t  y  t  b  n
s  r  g  m  s  h  h  s  k
a  p  o  s  o  m  a  t  e
d  r  u  m  m  i  n  g  s
d  e  u  e  e  n  k  e  b
t  l  e  a  p  e  t  a  l
```

**C.** Fill in the boxes with the right words.

1.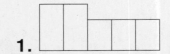

2.

3.

# Words with *th-*

| these | think | pretty |
|-------|-------|--------|
| those | thank | eight  |

## A. Use spelling words to complete the story.

One spring, the boys down the block saw baby ducks on their pond. They counted _____ of them swimming near the dock.

They had to _____ about how to make friends with ducks. They took bread to feed the ducks. When the ducks saw the boys on the dock, they swam away. The boys sat still for a very long time. They waited for the ducks to come back. The boys made friends with the baby ducks by feeding them and being very still. They fed them every day after school. Now _____ eight ducklings follow the boys everywhere.

## B. Write each word three times.

1. pretty _____ _____ _____

2. think _____ _____ _____

3. those _____ _____ _____

4. thank _____ _____ _____

5. these _____ _____ _____

6. eight _____ _____ _____

Name _____

# Words with *th-*

| | | |
|---|---|---|
| these | think | pretty |
| those | thank | eight |

**A.** Write each word two times in cursive.

*think*

*eight*

*pretty*

*those*

*these*

*thank*

**B.** Circle the word that is the same as the top one.

| think | pretty | these | eight | those | thank |
|---|---|---|---|---|---|
| thnik | preffy | those | eihgt | these | thank |
| think | prettg | tkese | ieght | fhose | think |
| thkin | pretty | thesc | eight | thosc | thnak |
| thunk | pnetty | these | eigth | those | thunk |

**C.** Finish the sentences.

1. I think _____.

2. That is a pretty _____.

| basket | rabbit | about |
|--------|--------|-------|
| blanket | visit | hive |

## A. Circle your spelling words.

1. Tell me about your grandmother.

2. I threw the ball into the basket.

3. Bees fly into the hive.

4. The animal with big ears was a rabbit.

5. We got an electric blanket for my bed.

6. I would like to visit my uncle.

## B. Fill in each blank with a spelling word.

1. Have you ever been to _____ the zoo?

2. We have a pet _____.

3. What is that story _____?

4. Put your dirty clothes in the laundry _____.

5. The _____ is full of bees.

6. I put a _____ on my bed when it was cold last week.

## C. Write a word that ends like each word below.

basket          hive          rabbit          about

_____      _____      _____      _____

Name _____     **61**

# Words with *-et* and *-it*

| | | |
|---|---|---|
| basket | rabbit | about |
| blanket | visit | hive |

**A.** Use spelling words to complete the story.

What a fine day for a picnic! Let's fill a _____ with good things to eat. I'll pack apples, cheese, fresh bread, and grapes. We'll _____ the spot in the woods by the stream. It is such a peaceful place.

I'll spread a _____ under an oak tree. Then we'll eat all our food. After that, we can skip rocks in the stream. And when we get tired, we'll lie in the shade and talk _____ this and that.

**B.** Fill in the boxes with the right words.

1.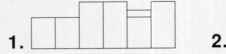

2.

3.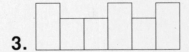

4.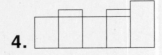

5.

6.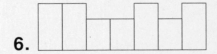

**C.** Put an *X* on the word that is <u>not</u> the same.

| 1. blanket | blanket | blanhet | blanket | blanket |
|---|---|---|---|---|
| 2. about | about | about | about | aboat |

# Words with -et and -it

| basket | rabbit | about |
|--------|--------|-------|
| blanket | visit | hive |

**A.** Write the spelling words in ABC order.

1. _____  2. _____  3. _____

4. _____  5. _____  6. _____

**B.** Write words that begin like each word below.

h̲ive      b̲asket      v̲isit      b̲lanket

_____   _____   _____   _____

_____   _____   _____   _____

_____   _____   _____   _____

**C.** Finish the sentences.

1. I will visit _____.

2. My pet rabbit _____.

3. The basket was full of _____.

**D.** Find the missing letters. Then write the word.

1. b _____ _____ _____ e t     _____

2. a b _____ _____ _____     _____

3. v i s _____ _____     _____

Name _____    **63**

# LESSON 16

## Words with *-et* and *-it*

| basket | rabbit | about |
|--------|--------|-------|
| blanket | visit | hive |

**A.** Circle the word that is the same as the top one.

| about | rabbit | basket | blanket | visit | hive |
|-------|--------|--------|---------|-------|------|
| aboat | rabdit | bisket | blanket | wisit | hvie |
| aboot | ribbet | basket | blonket | visit | hiev |
| about | rabbit | boshet | blinket | visif | hive |
| abuot | rabbif | bashet | blunket | visik | have |

**B.** Write each word two times in cursive.

*hive*

*basket*

*about*

*rabbit*

*visit*

*blanket*

**C.** Complete these exercises with spelling words.

1. Which word begins with two consonants? _____

2. Which word contains three vowels? _____

# Words with *-or* and *-om*

| doctor | bottom | use |
|--------|--------|-----|
| visitor | seldom | saw |

**A.** Circle your spelling words.

1. She drank the milk until she could see the bottom of the glass.

2. Do you know how to use a sled?

3. My friend was a visitor at our church.

4. We live so far away that we seldom get to see you.

5. When I had a bad cold, I went to see the doctor.

6. I saw you in the grocery store last Friday.

**B.** Write the spelling words in ABC order.

1. _____  2. _____  3. _____

4. _____  5. _____  6. _____

**C.** Fill in each blank with a spelling word.

1. My electric _____ cuts wood.

2. The _____ of my lunch bag fell out.

3. How many times have you been to the _____ this year?

4. We will have a _____ at school on Friday.

5. We _____ have duck for dinner.

Name _____

# Words with *-or* and *-om*

| doctor | bottom | use |
|--------|--------|-----|
| visitor | seldom | saw |

**A.** Use spelling words to complete the story.

My sister wanted to make a table. She bought some wood and nails. Since she _____ used a saw, she didn't have one of her own. So she used her friend's. But her friend's _____ was rusty. It had to be cleaned before it was ready to _____. My sister made a nice table. It's still in our kitchen. We eat at it each day.

**B.** Circle the word that is the same as the top one.

| doctor | visitor | bottom | seldom | use | saw |
|--------|---------|--------|--------|-----|-----|
| boctor | visitor | botton | saldom | vse | was |
| docfor | visiter | dottom | seldom | usc | sav |
| docton | viseter | buttom | suldom | use | sow |
| doctor | visater | bottom | soldom | nse | saw |

**C.** Finish the sentences.

1. We <u>seldom</u> go _____.

2. I know how to <u>use</u> _____.

# Words with *-or* and *-om*

| doctor | bottom | use |
|--------|--------|-----|
| visitor | seldom | saw |

**A.** Write each word two times in cursive.

*seldom*

*doctor*

*visitor*

*use*

*bottom*

*saw*

**B.** Write words that end like each word below.

doct<u>or</u>          botto<u>m</u>          sa<u>w</u>          us<u>e</u>

_____   _____   _____   _____

_____   _____   _____   _____

**C.** Fill in the boxes with the right words.

1. 

2. 

3. 

**D.** Finish the sentence.

I took the <u>visitor</u> _____.

Name _____

# Words with *-or* and *-om*

| | | |
|---|---|---|
| doctor | bottom | use |
| visitor | seldom | saw |

**A.** Find the hidden spelling words.

```
p  e  o  p  l  e  t  t  s  h  b
u  a  v  o  o  a  e  e  p  u  o
s  e  l  d  o  m  l  a  u  g  t
e  e  n  r  e  r  l  o  d  a  t
o  v  i  s  i  t  o  r  i  d  o
m  e  f  b  i  a  f  g  n  r  m
e  r  d  o  c  t  o  r  s  o  e
o  y  u  t  e  a  v  s  a  w  r
```

**B.** Write each word three times.

**1.** seldom _____ _____ _____

**2.** use _____ _____ _____

**3.** doctor _____ _____ _____

**4.** saw _____ _____ _____

**5.** visitor _____ _____ _____

**6.** bottom _____ _____ _____

**C.** Find the missing letters. Then write the word.

d _____ _____ _____ _____ _____      _____

# Words with *-ic* and *-ty*

| traffic | empty | say |
|---------|-------|-----|
| picnic | fifty | their |

**A. Circle your spelling words.**

1. It's a pretty day for a picnic.

2. The milk carton is empty.

3. The girls won their game today.

4. The traffic is bad downtown.

5. Two quarters is the same as fifty cents.

6. I'd like to say a few words.

**B. Fill in the boxes with the right words.**

1. 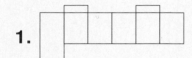 2.  3.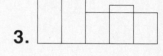

**C. Fill in each blank with a spelling word.**

1. Your stomach feels _____ when you are hungry.

2. How much did you _____ this cost?

3. At five o'clock the _____ is bad.

4. They got _____ new car today.

5. Let's take a _____ lunch to the park this afternoon.

Name _____

# LESSON 18

## Words with *-ic* and *-ty*

| traffic | empty | say |
|---------|-------|-----|
| picnic | fifty | their |

**A.** Write the spelling words in ABC order.

1. _____  2. _____  3. _____

4. _____  5. _____  6. _____

**B.** Circle the word that is the same as the top one.

| traffic | picnic | empty | fifty | their | say |
|---------|--------|-------|-------|-------|-----|
| lraffic | pacnic | empty | fefty | thier | saq |
| tnaffic | picnic | enpty | fofty | their | saw |
| traffic | picnoc | emqty | forty | thein | sav |
| treffic | pienic | emdty | fifty | fheir | say |

**C.** Find the missing letters. Then write the word.

1. t r ____ ____  f ____ ____      _____

2. p ____ ____  n ____ ____      _____

3. ____ m ____ ____ ____      _____

**D.** Use two of the spelling words in sentences.

1. _____

2. _____

70

| traffic | empty | say |
|---------|-------|-----|
| picnic | fifty | their |

**A.** Use spelling words to complete the story.

Our friends had a party in the park. _____ people came. We all brought _____ lunches. We played a game of baseball. Then it was time to eat.

"Hey, my lunch sack is _____!" cried a girl. I looked in my sack. It was empty, too. Then we saw a trail of food leading to the woods. "Let's see what got our food," I said. "What if it's a bear?" asked someone. We decided not to check the woods. People shared _____ food. We never knew what got into our sacks.

**B.** Write each word three times.

1. picnic _____ _____ _____

2. empty _____ _____ _____

3. their _____ _____ _____

**C.** Write these words from lessons before.

1. those _____      2. swimming _____

3. blanket _____      4. visit _____

5. doctor _____      6. seldom _____

Name _____

# LESSON 18

## Words with *-ic* and *-ty*

| traffic | empty | say |
|---------|-------|-----|
| picnic | fifty | their |

**A.** Write each word two times in cursive.

*fifty*

*picnic*

*traffic*

*empty*

*say*

*their*

**B.** Put an *X* on the word that is <u>not</u> the same.

| 1. | fifty | fifty | fifty | fitfy | fifty |
|----|-------|-------|-------|-------|-------|
| 2. | picnic | picnic | qicnic | picnic | picnic |
| 3. | their | their | their | their | thier |
| 4. | say | say | soy | say | say |
| 5. | traffic | traffic | traffic | tnaffic | traffic |

**C.** Fill in the boxes with the right words.

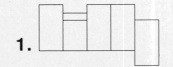 1.     2.    3.

72

# Words with *-le* and *-al*

| bottle | signal | been |
|--------|--------|------|
| candle | petal | before |

**A.** Circle your spelling words.

1. You must give a signal when you plan to turn.

2. The petal fell off the flower when I bumped it.

3. Use a match to light the candle.

4. Just before lunch, it began to rain.

5. I have been sick since yesterday.

6. The baby drinks from a bottle.

**B.** Fill in each blank with a spelling word.

1. The bee landed on a _____ of the rose.

2. Run for home plate when I give the _____.

3. Spring comes _____ summer.

4. Have you _____ doing all your work?

5. Which _____ of soda is yours?

6. If the lights go out, use a _____.

**C.** Write the spelling words in ABC order.

1. _____   2. _____   3. _____

4. _____   5. _____   6. _____

Name _____

# Words with *-le* and *-al*

| bottle | signal | been |
|--------|--------|------|
| candle | petal | before |

## A. Circle the word that is the same as the top one.

| bottle | been | candle | before | signal | petal |
|--------|------|--------|--------|--------|-------|
| battle | bean | candle | betore | sigral | betal |
| bittle | beeu | caudle | before | signal | batel |
| bottle | deen | cardle | befone | sigual | petal |
| bottel | been | cnadle | befoue | sigmal | detal |

## B. Use spelling words to complete the story.

It was dark outside and raining hard. I was trying to read a book. But the lights had _____ going on and off in the storm. So I found a _____. Then I got a match from the kitchen. I lit the candle.

_____ long, the lights went out and didn't come back on for the rest of the night. I was glad I had found the candle. I finished my book by the candle's light.

## C. Find the missing letters. Then write the word.

1. s _____ _____ n _____ l          _____

2. b e _____ _____ _____ e          _____

# Words with *-le* and *-al*

| bottle | signal | been |
|--------|--------|------|
| candle | petal | before |

**A.** Find the hidden spelling words.

```
b  t  l  e  a  p  e  t  a  l  s
e  e  u  a  d  b  a  o  n  e  i
f  a  n  t  d  o  t  s  y  s  g
o  c  c  y  e  t  i  s  o  s  n
r  h  h  o  d  t  n  o  n  o  a
e  r  b  s  o  l  b  e  e  n  l
d  i  e  u  i  e  e  n  v  s  p
a  g  a  c  a  n  d  l  e  o  e
y  n  s  e  d  i  o  t  r  u  n
```

**B.** Write each word three times.

**1.** candle _____ _____ _____

**2.** been _____ _____ _____

**3.** petal _____ _____ _____

**4.** bottle _____ _____ _____

**5.** before _____ _____ _____

**6.** signal _____ _____ _____

**C.** Finish the sentence.

Before Saturday, _____.

Name _____

# Words with *-le* and *-al*

| | | |
|---|---|---|
| bottle | signal | been |
| candle | petal | before |

## A. Write each word two times in cursive.

*bottle*

*been*

*signal*

*candle*

*petal*

*before*

## B. Put an *X* on the word that is <u>not</u> the same.

| 1. | bottle | bottle | bottle | battle | bottle |
|----|--------|--------|--------|--------|--------|
| 2. | been | been | beef | been | been |
| 3. | signal | signal | signal | signal | siqnal |
| 4. | candle | caudle | candle | candle | candle |
| 5. | petal | petal | pefal | petal | petal |

## C. Fill in the boxes with the right words.

1.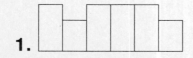

2.

3.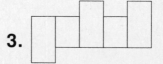

| melon | happily | mind |
|-------|---------|------|
| lemon | sadly | there |

**A.** **Circle your spelling words.**

1. A cantaloupe is a melon.

2. There is that sock I lost!

3. Do you mind if we watch a different show?

4. A lemon is very sour.

5. The baby played happily in his crib.

6. We sadly walked home when we couldn't find our dog.

**B.** **Fill in each blank with a spelling word.**

1. I like to eat ripe, sweet _____.

2. Do you _____ if I sit next to you?

3. I will _____ help you wash dishes.

4. The milk is over _____ on the table.

5. Do you like _____ in your iced tea?

6. She cried _____ when she did not do well on her spelling test.

**C.** **Write the spelling words in ABC order.**

1. _____    2. _____    3. _____

4. _____    5. _____    6. _____

Name _____

# Words with -on and -ly

| melon | happily | mind |
|-------|---------|------|
| lemon | sadly | there |

## A. Circle the word that is the same as the top one.

| lemon | there | sadly | melon | mind | happily |
|-------|-------|-------|-------|------|---------|
| lewon | tnere | sably | nelon | wind | happily |
| lemou | there | sadlv | meton | minb | hoppily |
| lemon | thore | sodly | melou | mind | heppily |
| lcmon | thare | sadly | melon | miud | happely |

## B. Use spelling words to complete the story.

My friend called early this morning. "Come see my new bike," he said. I ran _____ down the street to his house. He led me into the garage. "_____ it is," he said.

It was the best-looking bike I'd ever seen. I wanted one just like it. "Would you _____ if I took it for a ride?" I asked my friend.

## C. Find the missing letters. Then write the word.

1. _____ _____ e r e          _____

2. m _____ _____ _____          _____

# Words with *-on* and *-ly*

| melon | happily | mind |
|-------|---------|------|
| lemon | sadly | there |

**A.** Find the hidden spelling words.

```
b  n  s  t  f  b  y  e  m  h
h  e  l  f  h  a  m  g  a  s
a  t  h  e  r  e  o  a  f  a
p  h  o  o  t  l  a  p  a  d
p  m  i  n  d  e  a  t  l  l
i  s  p  r  o  m  p  t  l  y
l  s  p  a  c  o  r  u  e  o
y  m  e  l  o  n  a  r  t  u
a  i  a  a  f  o  y  k  u  t
```

**B.** Write each word three times.

1. happily _____ _____ _____

2. lemon _____ _____ _____

3. mind _____ _____ _____

4. melon _____ _____ _____

5. sadly _____ _____ _____

6. there _____ _____ _____

**C.** Finish the sentence.

This <u>lemon</u> is _____.

Name _____

# LESSON 20

## Words with *-on* and *-ly*

| melon | happily | mind |
|-------|---------|------|
| lemon | sadly | there |

**A.** Write each word two times in cursive.

*mind* _____

*melon* _____

*lemon* _____

*there* _____

*sadly* _____

*happily* _____

**B.** Fill in the boxes with the right words.

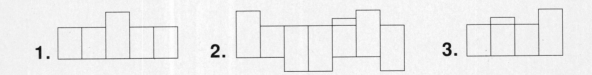

1.          2.          3.

**C.** Put an *X* on the word that is <u>not</u> the same.

| | | | | |
|---|---|---|---|---|
| **1.** sadly | sadly | sably | sadly | sadly |
| **2.** mind | mind | mind | mind | minb |
| **3.** there | thene | there | there | there |
| **4.** happily | happily | happily | hoppily | happily |

| studies | skate | carry |
|---------|-------|-------|
| studied | skin  | off   |

**A.** Circle your spelling words.

1. My friend studies all the time.

2. I studied my spelling and made an A on the test.

3. Do you like to skate?

4. I can't carry all these books.

5. Skin covers your bones.

6. Turn the lights off when you leave.

**B.** Fill in each blank with a spelling word.

1. Have you _____ your spelling words?

2. We scraped the ice _____ the windows.

3. Be careful not to sunburn your _____.

4. Will you _____ my books to class?

5. Do you like to _____ on ice?

6. I hope everyone _____ spelling each day.

**C.** Fill in the boxes with the right words.

1. 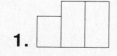 2. 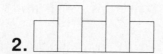 3.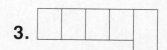

Name _____

# Words with *st-* and *sk-*

| | | |
|---|---|---|
| studies | skate | carry |
| studied | skin | off |

**A.** Write the spelling words in ABC order.

1. _____  2. _____  3. _____

4. _____  5. _____  6. _____

**B.** Use spelling words to complete the story.

Winter is my favorite time of year. The lake freezes over, and we go there to _____ on the ice. I like to go in the afternoon, when all my _____ are done.

We can even skate after dark. There are lights on the shore of the lake. The lights go _____ at eight. But by then, everyone is ready to go home and drink hot chocolate.

**C.** Circle the word that is the same as the top one.

| skate | off | carry | studies | skin | studied |
|-------|-----|-------|---------|------|---------|
| shate | oft | carvy | studies | shin | studies |
| skate | otf | carny | studied | skin | stubied |
| skaet | off | carrg | studics | skim | sfudied |
| skeat | ott | carry | sfudies | sken | studied |

# Words with *st-* and *sk-*

| studies | skate | carry |
|---------|-------|-------|
| studied | skin  | off   |

**A.** Find the hidden spelling words.

```
g r a s s e s e a t e d c
b a g b o a t h i s s b r
s k a t e a u a n e o o a
a s o a f b d m k n m f t
s l s t u d i e s t e f e
p a e o r f e m p t i e s
e m p t i e d a s k i n e
a e a e c a i n n e o d n
r n n c a r r y s y f s d
```

**B.** Write these words from lessons before.

**1.** signal _____        **2.** empty _____

**3.** plenty _____        **4.** lemon _____

**C.** Write each word three times.

**1.** carry _____ _____ _____

**2.** studies _____ _____ _____

**3.** off _____ _____ _____

**4.** studied _____ _____ _____

Name _____

# Words with *st-* and *sk-*

| studies | skate | carry |
|---------|-------|-------|
| studied | skin  | off   |

**A.** Write each word two times in cursive.

*skin*

*skate*

*carry*

*off*

*studies*

*studied*

**B.** Use two of the spelling words in sentences.

1. _____

2. _____

**C.** Put an X on the word that is not the same.

| 1. | off | off | off | oft | off |
|----|-----|-----|-----|-----|-----|
| 2. | studies | studies | stubies | studies | studies |
| 3. | carry | carny | carry | carry | carry |
| 4. | skin | skin | skin | skin | shin |
| 5. | skate | skate | skate | skute | skate |

# Words with *-ful*

| cupful | helpful | too |
|--------|---------|-----|
| handful | seven | under |

**A.** Circle your spelling words.

1. I am too sick to go to school today.

2. She put a handful of cookies in her lunch.

3. The recipe calls for a cupful of sugar.

4. I have seven sisters and brothers.

5. Are you helpful around the house?

6. The dog likes to sleep under the steps.

**B.** Fill in each blank with a spelling word.

1. My brother is _____ years old.

2. My sister is very _____ in the yard.

3. The box was _____ big to go through the door.

4. We got _____ the umbrella when the rain began.

5. Put a _____ of dirt over the seeds.

6. To make this cake, I need a _____ of flour.

**C.** Write the spelling words in ABC order.

1. _____    2. _____    3. _____

4. _____    5. _____    6. _____

Name _____

# Words with -ful

| | | |
|---|---|---|
| cupful | helpful | too |
| handful | seven | under |

**A.** Use spelling words to complete the story.

The young prince was unhappy being just a prince. "I want to be a great cook," he said. So he went to the palace cook for lessons. The cook told him to watch.

"Use a _____ of this and a _____ of that," she told him. Cooking looked _____ hard for the prince. "I think I'll find something easier to do," he said.

**B.** Circle the word that is the same as the top one.

| under | too | seven | handful | helpful | cupful |
|---|---|---|---|---|---|
| udner | foo | sever | bandful | helpful | oupful |
| umder | too | seven | nandful | helbful | copful |
| unber | toa | svene | handful | helbfnl | cubful |
| under | taa | sewer | dandful | helpfnl | cupful |

**C.** Find the missing letters. Then write the word.

1. c u ____ ____ ____ l _____

2. ____ ____ n d ____ ____ ____ _____

3. h e ____ ____ f ____ ____ _____

86

# Words with -ful

| | | |
|---|---|---|
| cupful | helpful | too |
| handful | seven | under |

**A.** Find the hidden spelling words.

```
y n s e d i o t r u n
t t o a s t r i p s p
r o s e v e n o p o e
o m o p o e c a e m o
o o m p n n e d c e p
t r e h e l p f u l l
o r s e e i u o p h e
o o o a s l f u f i p
l w u n d e r a u n a
s i h a n d f u l g p
o n o f f a o n a r e
a g a s e s f e e o e
```

**B.** Write each word three times.

1. seven _____ _____ _____

2. handful _____ _____ _____

3. helpful _____ _____ _____

4. cupful _____ _____ _____

5. too _____ _____ _____

6. under _____ _____ _____

Name _____

# Words with -ful

| cupful | helpful | too |
|--------|---------|-----|
| handful | seven | under |

**A.** Write each word two times in cursive.

*helpful*

*seven*

*handful*

*cupful*

*under*

*too*

**B.** Put an *X* on the word that is <u>not</u> the same.

| **1.** under | under | unber | under | under |
|---|---|---|---|---|
| **2.** seven | seven | seven | seven | sever |
| **3.** too | too | too | too | foo |
| **4.** helpful | helptul | helpful | helpful | helpful |

**C.** Fill in the boxes with the right words.

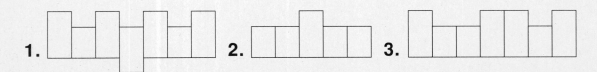

1.    2.    3.

# Words with *sh-*

| shall | shell | want |
|-------|-------|------|
| shack | shelf | first |

**A.** Circle your spelling words.

  **1.** The man lives in a shack in the woods.

  **2.** We keep the cans up on the shelf.

  **3.** How much salad do you want?

  **4.** I was first in the lunch line today.

  **5.** I found a shell on the beach.

  **6.** How much shall I charge for this scarf?

**B.** Fill in each blank with a spelling word.

  **1.** I found a pretty _____ at the beach.

  **2.** Do you _____ to go to the movies?

  **3.** We keep our tools in a _____ outside.

  **4.** Put the books back on the _____.

  **5.** How often _____ I take out the trash?

  **6.** Who came in _____ in the three-legged race?

**C.** Write the spelling words in ABC order.

  **1.** _____   **2.** _____   **3.** _____

  **4.** _____   **5.** _____   **6.** _____

Name _____

# Words with *sh-*

| | | |
|---|---|---|
| shall | shell | want |
| shack | shelf | first |

**A.** Use spelling words to complete the story.

I love to walk on the beach. You should see what I find there. Once I found a _____ that looked like an ear. There was a hole in it, so I made the shell into a necklace.

I also have three perfect sand dollars. I _____ to show off all my shells. But _____ I need to build a _____ to put them on.

**B.** Circle the word that is the same as the top one.

| want | first | shack | shell | shelf | shall |
|------|-------|-------|-------|-------|-------|
| went | finst | shack | skell | shelt | shell |
| wont | firsf | shuck | shell | shelf | sholl |
| want | tirst | shock | shall | shalf | shall |
| what | first | snack | shcll | sholf | snall |

**C.** Put an X on the word that is <u>not</u> the same.

| 1. | shall | shall | shell | shall | shall |
|----|-------|-------|-------|-------|-------|
| 2. | want | wart | want | want | want |
| 3. | first | first | first | finst | first |

# Words with sh-

| shall | shell | want |
|-------|-------|------|
| shack | shelf | first |

**A.** Find the hidden spelling words.

```
s m e l o n a r t u b n s
s t e e r r h w a n t a b
s l e e p a o e p o e l s
h e a r o s r a p r n l h
a m n b c h s t l t l a a
l r o o v s e h e h e u c
l o n g b h e e s s s g k
a v e n u e l r w i s h r
a s t a l l f s h e l l k
b l u e o f f i r s t w i
s o m e m e e t r b s v d
a s p a c o r u e o a i a
```

**B.** Write each word three times.

1. shall _____  _____  _____

2. want _____  _____  _____

3. shack _____  _____  _____

4. first _____  _____  _____

5. shell _____  _____  _____

6. shelf _____  _____  _____

Name _____

# LESSON 23

## Words with *sh-*

| | | |
|---|---|---|
| shall | shell | want |
| shack | shelf | first |

**A.** Write each word two times in cursive.

*shack* _____

*shell* _____

*shelf* _____

*shall* _____

*first* _____

*want* _____

**B.** Fill in the boxes with the right words.

1. 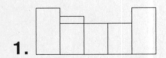     2. 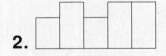     3.

4. 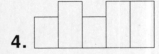     5.     6.

**C.** Find the missing letters. Then write the word.

1. ____ ____ a c k          _____

2. ____ ____ e l f          _____

3. w a ____ ____          _____

92

# Words with *sh-*

| ship | shock | both |
|------|-------|------|
| shift | shop | does |

**A.** Circle your spelling words.

1. Do you like to shop at the grocery store?

2. Where does your mother work?

3. Do you know how to drive a car with a stick shift?

4. Don't touch the wire or you might get a shock.

5. That ship goes across the ocean.

6. Raise both arms at the same time.

**B.** Fill in each blank with a spelling word.

1. If you touch the light switch with wet hands, you might

   get a _____.

2. Do you know how to _____ the gears in a car?

3. My mother went to _____ for a new coat.

4. This woman is the captain of the _____.

5. Look _____ ways before you cross the street.

**C.** Use two of the spelling words in sentences.

1. _____

2. _____

Name _____

# Words with *sh-*

| ship | shock | both |
|------|-------|------|
| shift | shop | does |

**A. Use spelling words to complete the story.**

Remember my friend who got a new bike? Boy, was he in

for a _____. The bike had ten gears. It took him a

week to learn to _____ them all. "They didn't tell me

about this at the _____," he said.

But he soon learned to ride like a champ. He even learned

how to fix the bike if it breaks.

**B. Circle the word that is the same as the top one.**

| both | shift | does | ship | shock | shop |
|------|-------|------|------|-------|------|
| bath | chift | doez | ship | shack | ship |
| bafh | shlft | boes | shop | shuck | shop |
| doth | shift | deos | shap | shock | shob |
| both | shiff | does | skip | shoch | skop |

**C. Finish the sentences.**

1. I like to <u>shop</u> _____.

2. <u>Both</u> of the girls _____.

# Words with *sh-*

| | | |
|---|---|---|
| ship | shock | both |
| shift | shop | does |

**A.** Find the hidden spelling words.

```
s a v s a h t y r a a o
s d a r k e w s e e m y
h f l e e a h h i l l e
i m a n y s o i l e t s
f o o i s h o p f l d g
t o f f e o i a a a o i
b d r p a c l c s m e r
l b o t h k l k t b s l
a e a e e s e e a b e b
```

**B.** Write each word three times.

**1.** shop  _____  _____  _____

**2.** both  _____  _____  _____

**3.** ship  _____  _____  _____

**4.** does  _____  _____  _____

**C.** Write these words from lessons before.

**1.** flute  _____      **2.** studies  _____

**3.** cupful  _____      **4.** want  _____

Name _____

# Words with *sh-*

| | | |
|---|---|---|
| ship | shock | both |
| shift | shop | does |

**A.** Write each word two times in cursive.

*shock*

*shop*

*shift*

*ship*

*both*

*does*

**B.** Put an *X* on the word that is <u>not</u> the same.

| | | | | |
|---|---|---|---|---|
| **1.** both | bath | both | both | both |
| **2.** ship | ship | ship | skip | ship |
| **3.** shop | shop | shop | shop | snop |
| **4.** does | does | boes | does | does |
| **5.** shock | shock | shock | shoch | shock |

**C.** Fill in the boxes with the right words.

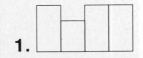 1.          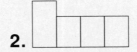 2.          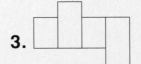 3.

# Words with *wh-*

| | | |
|---|---|---|
| what | which | thunder |
| white | when | shut |

## A. Circle your spelling words.

1. Have you ever seen a white rose?

2. Please shut the door.

3. I think it is going to thunder.

4. What is your name?

5. I can't tell which book is mine.

6. When do you go to bed?

## B. Fill in each blank with a spelling word.

1. _____ house is yours?

2. Please _____ all the windows, because it is going to rain.

3. The _____ woke me up in the middle of the night.

4. _____ time is it?

5. _____ will it be time to eat?

6. Snow is _____.

## C. Use two of the spelling words in sentences.

1. _____

2. _____

Name _____

# Words with *wh-*

| what | which | thunder |
|------|-------|---------|
| white | when | shut |

**A.** Write words that begin like each word below.

w̲hat        s̲hut        t̲hunder

_____    _____    _____

_____    _____    _____

**B.** Circle the word that is the same as the top one.

| white | which | what | when | shut | thunder |
|-------|-------|------|------|------|---------|
| mhite | whach | whot | whin | snut | thumber |
| whlitt | whuch | whaf | when | shut | thunder |
| white | which | mhat | whun | shnt | thunber |
| wnite | whoch | what | whon | shuf | thnuder |

**C.** Write the spelling words that rhyme with the words below.

**1.** nut    cut    _____

**2.** ten    pen    _____

**3.** bite    kite    _____

**D.** Find the missing letters. Then write the word.

t h _____ _____ d e r    _____

# Words with *wh-*

| | | |
|---|---|---|
| what | which | thunder |
| white | when | shut |

**A.** Use spelling words to complete the story.

My dog Buff is afraid of loud noises. He's especially afraid

of _____. It makes him shake all over. He hides

under the bed _____ there's a storm. I asked the vet

_____ to do about Buff. "Pat him and talk to him in

a soft voice," she said.

But this didn't seem to help. Then I got an idea. The next

time there was a storm, I got the headphones for my radio. I

put them on Buff's ears. It worked! He didn't shake or hide

under the bed.

**B.** Write the spelling words in ABC order.

1. _____    2. _____    3. _____

4. _____    5. _____    6. _____

**C.** Write each word three times.

1. shut    _____  _____  _____

2. white   _____  _____  _____

3. what    _____  _____  _____

4. thunder _____  _____  _____

Name _____

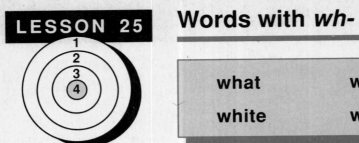

# LESSON 25

## Words with *wh-*

| what | which | thunder |
|------|-------|---------|
| white | when | shut |

**A.** Write each word two times in cursive.

*what*

*white*

*shut*

*which*

*when*

*thunder*

**B.** Put an *X* on the word that is <u>not</u> the same.

| 1. when | when | when | whan | when |
|---------|------|------|------|------|
| 2. shut | shut | shuf | shut | shut |
| 3. what | what | what | what | wkat |
| 4. white | whife | white | white | white |

**C.** Fill in the boxes with the right words.

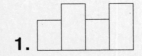 1.    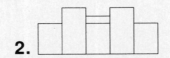 2.    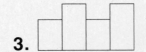 3.

# Words with *ch-*

| chat | check | with |
|------|-------|------|
| champ | chest | yes |

**A.** Circle your spelling words.

1. Inside your chest are your ribs.

2. I hope you say yes when I ask this question.

3. We had a nice chat on the telephone.

4. Do you like to play with me?

5. She is the jump rope champ in our group.

6. Please check my paper.

**B.** Fill in each blank with a spelling word.

1. I am the spelling _____ of my class.

2. Sit down and _____ with me for a while.

3. Will you come play tennis _____ me?

4. I paid for the dress by _____.

5. I keep my clothes in a _____ of drawers.

6. _____, you may have some orange juice.

**C.** Find the missing letters. Then write the word.

1. ____ i t h                _____

2. ____ ____ a t             _____

Name _____                **101**

# Words with *ch-*

| chat | check | with |
|------|-------|------|
| champ | chest | yes |

**A.** Write words that begin like each word below.

<u>y</u>es       <u>ch</u>at       <u>w</u>ith

_____    _____    _____

_____    _____    _____

**B.** Write the spelling words in ABC order.

1. _____  2. _____  3. _____

4. _____  5. _____  6. _____

**C.** Fill in each blank with a spelling word.

1. Did you write this _____ with your own pen?

2. I'd like to have a _____ with you soon.

**D.** Circle the word that is the same as the top one.

| <u>chat</u> | <u>with</u> | <u>yes</u> | <u>champ</u> | <u>check</u> | <u>chest</u> |
|------|------|-----|-------|-------|-------|
| cnat | mith | yez | chomp | sheck | chist |
| chaf | with | yos | chump | check | chest |
| chat | wtih | yus | champ | chock | chost |
| cbat | whit | yes | chimp | cheek | cnest |

# Words with *ch-*

| | | |
|---|---|---|
| chat | check | with |
| champ | chest | yes |

**A.** Write each word two times in cursive.

*with*

*yes*

*champ*

*chat*

*check*

*chest*

**B.** Use two of the spelling words in sentences.

1. _____

2. _____

**C.** Fill in the boxes with the right words.

1.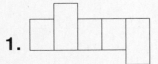

2.

3.

4.

5.

6.

Name _____

# Words with *ch-*

| chat | check | with |
|------|-------|------|
| champ | chest | yes |

**A.** Use spelling words to complete the story.

The _____ of the boxing match went to the locker

room to rest. But the fans wanted to see him. "Please

_____ with me in five minutes," the boxer told the

people. "I need to catch my breath."

Finally, the fans went in to see the champ. They were so

proud of him. The champ was glad to visit _____ his

fans.

**B.** Write the spelling words that rhyme with the words below.

**1.** cat        sat        _____

**2.** camp     stamp     _____

**3.** best      rest       _____

**C.** Write each word three times.

**1.** chat      _____    _____    _____

**2.** champ    _____    _____    _____

**3.** with      _____    _____    _____

**4.** yes       _____    _____    _____

# Words with *tw-* and *qu-*

| twin | quit | who |
|------|------|-----|
| twenty | quick | will |

**A.** Circle your spelling words.

1. My sister quit taking tennis lessons.

2. My twin brother and I look alike.

3. I will not be on time for school.

4. Who is going to shop with you?

5. My friend is a very quick runner.

6. Twenty people came to my birthday party.

**B.** Fill in each blank with a spelling word.

1. _____ takes you to school?

2. Which girl is your _____ sister?

3. This is a _____ pie to make.

4. I _____ not be able to go to the picnic.

5. I cannot wait until I am _____ years old.

6. I wish you would _____ tickling me.

**C.** Use two of the spelling words in sentences.

1. _____

2. _____

Name _____

# Words with *tw-* and *qu-*

| twin | quit | who |
|------|------|-----|
| twenty | quick | will |

**A.** Write words that begin like each word below.

who                will                quit

_____        _____        _____

_____        _____        _____

**B.** Write the spelling words in ABC order.

1. _____  2. _____  3. _____

4. _____  5. _____  6. _____

**C.** Circle the word that is the same as the top one.

| quick | who | twin | twenty | quit | will |
|-------|-----|------|--------|------|------|
| quiet | how | tmin | twenty | puit | mill |
| quict | who | twim | twinty | quit | wall |
| guick | mho | twen | twemty | gnit | will |
| quick | wno | twin | twumty | qnit | wilt |

**D.** Find the missing letters. Then write the word.

1. w h _____                    _____

2. t w _____ _____ t _____      _____

# Words with *tw-* and *qu-*

| twin | quit | who |
|------|------|-----|
| twenty | quick | will |

**A.** Write each word two times in cursive.

*who* _____

*will* _____

*twin* _____

*twenty* _____

*quit* _____

*quick* _____

**B.** Use spelling words to complete the story.

    The twins liked to play tricks on people. They looked exactly

alike. They always wore the same kind of clothes. Only their

parents could tell _____ was who. At school they

would change places and fool their teachers and friends.

    "_____ teasing us," their friends would demand.

"Now tell us, _____ you, which one is which?"

    Each twin would use the other twin's name. Pretty soon,

even they were mixed up. "Are you me, or am I you?" they

would ask each other.

Name _____

# Words with *tw-* and *qu-*

| | | |
|---|---|---|
| twin | quit | who |
| twenty | quick | will |

**A.** Find the hidden spelling words.

```
s n e d e d s o p s
n m i n d e a t l l
o w w e e q u i c k
t h i p t u m c o e
w o l o e i b i d y
i e l l m t r n r s
n e e d s h e g i o
u v a r o o l c n m
m e c e m u l a k e
t w e n t y a k k o
e y o m o a r e e n
r i n e n n t s e e
```

**B.** Write each word three times.

1. will  _____  _____  _____

2. who  _____  _____  _____

3. quit  _____  _____  _____

4. twenty  _____  _____  _____

5. quick  _____  _____  _____

6. twin  _____  _____  _____

© 1991 Steck-Vaughn Company. Target 360

## LESSON 28  Words with *-ch, -sh,* and *-ng*

| | | |
|---|---|---|
| bunch | flash | hang |
| lunch | cash | sang |

**A.** Circle your spelling words.

1. I saw a flash of lightning.

2. This is a bunch of grapes.

3. We eat lunch at noon.

4. They paid cash for the dresses.

5. We sang a song on his birthday.

6. Please hang up your clothes.

**B.** Fill in each blank with a spelling word.

1. Let's eat pizza for _____.

2. I gave you ten dollars in _____.

3. Do you like to work with _____ cards?

4. A _____ of my friends went swimming.

5. The boy likes to _____ upside down.

6. The girls _____ a funny song.

**C.** Write the spelling words in ABC order.

1. _____  2. _____  3. _____

4. _____  5. _____  6. _____

Name _____  **109**

# Words with *-ch, -sh,* and *-ng*

| bunch | flash | hang |
|-------|-------|------|
| lunch | cash | sang |

**A.** Circle the word that is the same as the top one.

| lunch | cash | bunch | hang | sang | flash |
|-------|------|-------|------|------|-------|
| lunck | cask | bunch | hnag | snag | flash |
| lunkc | eash | bunhc | hang | sung | flask |
| lunhc | cash | bunkc | hung | sang | flasr |
| lunch | casn | bunck | hong | sing | tlash |

**B.** Write words that begin like each word below.

c̲ash          b̲unch          f̲lash          h̲ang

_____     _____     _____     _____

_____     _____     _____     _____

**C.** Fill in the boxes with the right words.

1. 

2. 

3. 

**D.** Find the missing letters. Then write the word.

**1.** h _____ _____ _____          _____

**2.** b _____ n _____ _____          _____

# Words with *-ch, -sh,* and *-ng*

| bunch | flash | hang |
|-------|-------|------|
| lunch | cash | sang |

**A.** Write each word two times in cursive.

*hang*

*lunch*

*bunch*

*cash*

*flash*

*sang*

**B.** Use two of the spelling words in sentences.

1. _____

2. _____

**C.** Put an *X* on the word that is <u>not</u> the same.

| 1. | cash | cash | cash | cask | cash |
|----|------|------|------|------|------|
| 2. | lunch | lunch | lunck | lunch | lunch |
| 3. | bunch | bunck | bunch | bunch | bunch |
| 4. | hang | hang | hang | hank | hang |
| 5. | flash | flasn | flash | flash | flash |

Name _____

# Words with *-ch, -sh,* and *-ng*

| bunch | flash | hang |
|-------|-------|------|
| lunch | cash | sang |

**A.** Use spelling words to complete the story.

One Saturday I invited my friends over for _____.

When I looked in the kitchen, I saw we needed some things

to eat. So I went to the store to buy food. We needed bread,

chips, fruit, and sodas. When it was time to pay, I got out my

wallet. But the wallet had no _____.

"Please hold this food for me," I said to the man at the

store. "I'll run home for some money and be back in a

_____."

**B.** Write the spelling words that rhyme with the words below.

1. bunch    crunch    _____

2. dash    cash    _____

3. bang    rang    _____

**C.** Write each word three times.

1. lunch    _____    _____    _____

2. hang    _____    _____    _____

3. bunch    _____    _____    _____

4. flash    _____    _____    _____

# Words with -sh

| fresh | wish | because |
|-------|------|---------|
| flesh | dish | always |

**A.** Circle your spelling words.

1. I love fresh strawberries.

2. She is always happy.

3. He is sad because his dog is sick.

4. I wish it were summer.

5. Please buy the dog a food dish.

6. The meat of an animal is called flesh.

**B.** Fill in each blank with a spelling word.

1. Before you blow out candles on a birthday cake, you

   make a _____.

2. To see if the fish was done, we stuck a fork in its _____.

3. We are having _____ green beans for dinner.

4. You are _____ nice to be around.

5. I like you _____ you are fun.

6. I dropped a _____ on the floor and broke it.

**C.** Finish the sentence.

I wish _____.

Name _____

# Words with -sh

| fresh | wish | because |
|-------|------|---------|
| flesh | dish | always |

**A.** Circle the word that is the same as the top one.

| fresh | because | wish | always | flesh | dish |
|-------|---------|------|--------|-------|------|
| flesh | becavse | wash | alvays | flesh | dash |
| frehs | because | wish | alwavs | flash | disk |
| fresh | becanse | with | almays | tlesh | dish |
| fnesh | decause | wihs | always | flush | dizh |

**B.** Use spelling words to complete the story.

One night I said to my friend, "Let's have _____ fish

for supper. We can catch the fish in the lake. Then we can

cook it on the grill."

We fished for a long time. My friend said, "I _____

we would catch a catfish. Catfish is _____ good to eat."

I said, "Wait a little longer. We'll catch a fish soon!" At dark,

we still had no fish. So we gave up and walked sadly home.

**C.** Find the missing letters. Then write the word.

1. w _____ _____ _____     _____

2. _____ r _____ s h     _____

# LESSON 29    Words with -sh

| fresh | wish | because |
|-------|------|---------|
| flesh | dish | always |

**A.** Write each word two times in cursive.

*fresh*

*flesh*

*because*

*wish*

*dish*

*always*

**B.** Fill in the boxes with the right words.

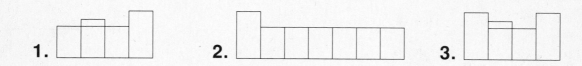

1.     2.     3.

**C.** Put an *X* on the word that is <u>not</u> the same.

| 1. dish | dish | dish | dish | disk |
|---------|------|------|------|------|
| 2. because | because | becuase | because | because |
| 3. fresh | fresh | fnesh | fresh | fresh |
| 4. always | always | always | almays | always |
| 5. flesh | flesh | flcsh | flesh | flesh |

Name _____    **115**

# LESSON 29

1
2
3
4

## Words with -sh

| fresh | wish | because |
| flesh | dish | always |

**A.** Find the hidden spelling words.

```
b s h o w i n d o w
e h i s a a m s o i
c h f g l n e e n s
a a a l w f l e s h
u m l a a d o t s a
s p l a y i v a a n
e o f e s s e l n y
i f r e s h r w d e
t o i a o o o a r s
```

**B.** Write each word three times.

1. dish _____ _____ _____

2. because _____ _____ _____

3. fresh _____ _____ _____

4. always _____ _____ _____

5. wish _____ _____ _____

6. flesh _____ _____ _____

**C.** Finish the sentence.

I always _____.

116

# Words with -sh

| | | |
|---|---|---|
| crush | rush | were |
| brush | hush | table |

**A.** Circle your spelling words.

1. I forgot to brush my hair.

2. We had to rush home.

3. Please put the books on the table.

4. When you want someone to be quiet, you say "hush."

5. Our blender can crush ice.

6. They were at home when the lights went out.

**B.** Fill in each blank with a spelling word.

1. When you are in a big hurry, you _____ home.

2. My sister told me to _____, because she was trying to do her homework.

3. We _____ late getting to the movie.

4. When I _____ ice, it makes a loud noise.

5. Would you like to sit at the _____?

6. Don't forget to _____ your teeth.

**C.** Write the spelling words in ABC order.

1. _____  2. _____  3. _____

4. _____  5. _____  6. _____

Name _____

# LESSON 30 — Words with *-sh*

| crush | rush | were |
|-------|------|------|
| brush | hush | table |

## A. Circle the word that is the same as the top one.

| crush | were | brush | hush | rush | table |
|-------|------|-------|------|------|-------|
| crash | wene | drush | hash | rush | tadle |
| cnash | werc | brush | hnsh | rusn | tablc |
| cnush | were | drnsh | shuh | rash | fable |
| crush | mere | brash | hush | rusk | table |

## B. Use spelling words to complete the story.

You should have seen us before our vacation. We

_____ all running late. Our plane was to leave at

nine in the morning. We were in such a _____ that

we just left our breakfast dishes in the sink.

On the way out the front door, my sister said, "I forgot my

_____!" At last we jumped in the car and sped to

the airport. We got on the plane just in time.

## C. Fill in the boxes with the right words.

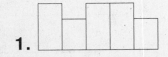

1.    2.    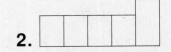 3.

118

# Words with -sh

| crush | rush | were |
|-------|------|------|
| brush | hush | table |

**A.** Write each word two times in cursive.

*brush* _____

*rush* _____

*hush* _____

*table* _____

*were* _____

*crush* _____

**B.** Write these words from lessons before.

**1.** check _____    **2.** because _____

**3.** which _____    **4.** wish _____

**5.** quick _____    **6.** flesh _____

**C.** Use four of the spelling words in sentences.

**1.** _____

**2.** _____

**3.** _____

**4.** _____

Name _____

# Words with -sh

| crush | rush | were |
|-------|------|------|
| brush | hush | table |

**A.** Find the hidden spelling words.

```
q  a  s  n  g  a  s  k  e
c  b  a  c  k  d  s  y  h
v  r  r  r  e  r  e  e  u
a  o  e  u  e  e  e  s  s
t  w  a  s  p  s  b  t  h
w  n  n  h  i  l  r  a  l
e  b  i  e  n  e  u  b  i
r  l  m  a  g  s  s  l  t
e  u  a  r  u  s  h  e  t
b  e  l  i  r  e  a  a  l
```

**B.** Write words that end like each word below.

brush                    table                    were

_____    _____    _____

_____    _____    _____

**C.** Write each word three times.

**1.** were    _____    _____    _____

**2.** rush    _____    _____    _____

**3.** crush    _____    _____    _____

# My Word List

## Words I Can Spell

Put a ✓ in the box beside each word you spell correctly on your weekly test.

### 1

- ☐ bled
- ☐ block
- ☐ black
- ☐ blind
- ☐ woman
- ☐ wonder

### 2

- ☐ glad
- ☐ glass
- ☐ flag
- ☐ flip
- ☐ many
- ☐ wash

### 3

- ☐ plant
- ☐ plus
- ☐ slept
- ☐ slid
- ☐ small
- ☐ try

### 4

- ☐ scalp
- ☐ scan
- ☐ scrub
- ☐ scribble
- ☐ plenty
- ☐ brown

### 5

- ☐ skill
- ☐ skunk
- ☐ snap
- ☐ snack
- ☐ flute
- ☐ goes

## Words To Review

If you miss a word on your test, write it here. Practice it until you can spell it correctly. Then check the box beside the word.

_____

_____

_____

_____

_____

_____

_____

_____

_____

_____

_____

_____

_____

_____

Name _____

# My Word List

## Words I Can Spell

Put a ✓ in the box beside each word you spell correctly on your weekly test.

### 6

☐ spend          ☐ stamp

☐ spill          ☐ never

☐ study          ☐ warm

### 7

☐ swing          ☐ arm

☐ swim           ☐ book

☐ swimming       ☐ four

### 8

☐ crust          ☐ myself

☐ crack          ☐ much

☐ crash          ☐ kind

### 9

☐ drum           ☐ grab

☐ drink          ☐ frog

☐ grass          ☐ done

### 10

☐ prompt         ☐ strap

☐ press          ☐ group

☐ string         ☐ laugh

## Words To Review

If you miss a word on your test, write it here. Practice it until you can spell it correctly. Then check the box beside the word.

_____

_____

_____

_____

_____

_____

_____

_____

_____

_____

_____

_____

_____

# My Word List

## Words I Can Spell

Put a ✓ in the box beside each word you spell correctly on your weekly test.

### 11

☐ trip  ☐ class

☐ trust  ☐ again

☐ club  ☐ after

### 12

☐ drank  ☐ junk

☐ bank  ☐ inch

☐ trunk  ☐ pinch

### 13

☐ branch  ☐ strung

☐ ranch  ☐ together

☐ swung  ☐ today

### 14

☐ wink  ☐ dollar

☐ blink  ☐ full

☐ collar  ☐ hurt

### 15

☐ these  ☐ thank

☐ those  ☐ pretty

☐ think  ☐ eight

## Words To Review

If you miss a word on your test, write it here. Practice it until you can spell it correctly. Then check the box beside the word.

Name _____

# My Word List

## Words I Can Spell

Put a ✓ in the box beside each word you spell correctly on your weekly test.

### 16

- ☐ basket
- ☐ blanket
- ☐ rabbit
- ☐ visit
- ☐ about
- ☐ hive

### 17

- ☐ doctor
- ☐ visitor
- ☐ bottom
- ☐ seldom
- ☐ use
- ☐ saw

### 18

- ☐ traffic
- ☐ picnic
- ☐ empty
- ☐ fifty
- ☐ say
- ☐ their

### 19

- ☐ bottle
- ☐ candle
- ☐ signal
- ☐ petal
- ☐ been
- ☐ before

### 20

- ☐ melon
- ☐ lemon
- ☐ happily
- ☐ sadly
- ☐ mind
- ☐ there

## Words To Review

If you miss a word on your test, write it here. Practice it until you can spell it correctly. Then check the box beside the word.

_____

_____

_____

_____

_____

_____

_____

_____

_____

_____

_____

_____

_____

_____

_____

# My Word List

## Words I Can Spell

Put a ✓ in the box beside each word you spell correctly on your weekly test.

### 21

- ☐ studies
- ☐ studied
- ☐ skate
- ☐ skin
- ☐ carry
- ☐ off

### 22

- ☐ cupful
- ☐ handful
- ☐ helpful
- ☐ seven
- ☐ too
- ☐ under

### 23

- ☐ shall
- ☐ shack
- ☐ shell
- ☐ shelf
- ☐ want
- ☐ first

### 24

- ☐ ship
- ☐ shift
- ☐ shock
- ☐ shop
- ☐ both
- ☐ does

### 25

- ☐ what
- ☐ white
- ☐ which
- ☐ when
- ☐ thunder
- ☐ shut

## Words To Review

If you miss a word on your test, write it here. Practice it until you can spell it correctly. Then check the box beside the word.

_____

_____

_____

_____

_____

_____

_____

_____

_____

_____

_____

_____

Name _____

# My Word List

## Words I Can Spell

Put a ✓ in the box beside each word you spell correctly on your weekly test.

### 26

☐ chat      ☐ chest
☐ champ     ☐ with
☐ check     ☐ yes

### 27

☐ twin      ☐ quick
☐ twenty    ☐ who
☐ quit      ☐ will

### 28

☐ bunch     ☐ cash
☐ lunch     ☐ hang
☐ flash     ☐ sang

### 29

☐ fresh     ☐ dish
☐ flesh     ☐ because
☐ wish      ☐ always

### 30

☐ crush     ☐ hush
☐ brush     ☐ were
☐ rush      ☐ table

## Words To Review

If you miss a word on your test, write it here. Practice it until you can spell it correctly. Then check the box beside the word.

_____

_____

_____

_____

_____

_____

_____

_____

_____

_____

_____

_____

_____

_____